Super-sub Stingray of the World ~~Aquanaut Security~~ Patrol (WASPS) is the spe~~arhe~~ad of the world ~~s~~ defence against the hostile undersea races who are trying to take over the land. Anything can happen in the next 62 pages.

Editor: Alan Fennell   Design: Cally Stewart

£4.75

STINGRAY

THE CONTROL TOWER, MARINEVILLE...

GET THIS INFORMATION OVER THE SCRAMBLER TO THE RIO DE JANEIRO BASE, LIEUTENANT FISHER.

YES, SIR.

OPEN CHANNEL SIXTEEN. CLASSIFIED MATERIAL COMING OVER.

CHANNEL OPEN, LIEUTENANT. FIRE AWAY.

SECONDS LATER, RIO DE JANEIRO REPORTS BACK TO MARINEVILLE...

SAY, MARINEVILLE, IS THIS SOME KIND OF JOKE? I CAN'T FIGURE OUT WHAT'S COMING OVER THE SCRAMBLER!

HANG ON... I'LL REPEAT THE LAST DOCUMENT.

WHAT'S THE TROUBLE, FISHER?

THE SCRAMBLER APPEARS TO HAVE GONE HAYWIRE, COMMANDER.

MESSAGE STILL UNINTELLIGIBLE, LIEUTENANT.

CHECK OUT ALL SYSTEMS... IT SEEMS INCREDIBLE, BUT SOMEONE OR SOMETHING MUST BE INTERFERING WITH THE TRICO WAVE LENGTH.

MEANWHILE, ACROSS THE SOUTH AMERICAN CONTINENT, MONO-RAIL HISTORY IS BEING MADE...

LADIES AND GENTLEMEN, WE ARE SPEEDING THROUGH THIS PRIMITIVE SCENERY AT THREE HUNDRED MILES AN HOUR.

INSIDE A MONO-RAIL COMPARTMENT A WORLD T.V. CAMERA CREW IS IN ACTION...

MR. RYAN, THIS IS A MIGHTY HAPPY DAY FOR YOU. THERE MUST HAVE BEEN TIMES WHEN YOU THOUGHT YOU'D NEVER COMPLETE THIS AMAZON RUN.

WE SURE HAD OUR QUOTA OF BAD LUCK, BUT TODAY MAKES UP FOR ALL THAT. WE KNOW THE CONSTRUCTION IS PERFECT.

BUT FIVE HUNDRED MILES FURTHER DOWN THE TRACK ALIEN CREATURES PLAN TO WRECK RYAN'S EFFORTS!

YOU MUST HURRY! THE SURFACE CREATURE'S MACHINE IS AHEAD OF SCHEDULE ACCORDING TO THE SCANNERS...

MY WORK IS COMPLETE! WE ARE READY TO RETURN TO THE LAKE.

THE TWO ALIENS REACH THEIR CRAFT AND PREPARE FOR LAUNCH...

SURFACE PARTY RETURNING TO BASE.

THE STRANGE CRAFT TAKES OFF...

YOU HAVE DONE A GOOD JOB. THE SURFACE MEN MUST NEVER KNOW OF OUR EXISTENCE OR IT WILL BE OUR END.

AND SOON PLUNGES INTO THE DEPTHS OF THE AMAZON...

...MEANWHILE, AT MARINEVILLE, LIEUTENANT FISHER REPORTS TO COMMANDER SHORE...

THERE'S NO FAULT IN THE SCRAMBLER EQUIPMENT AT ALL, SIR...THE ENGINEERS MAINTAIN THAT THE IRREGULAR MESSAGES RECEIVED AT RIO MUST BE A SIGNAL ON THE SAME WAVE LENGTH BUTTING IN...

BUT WHO IN THE NAME OF THUNDER WOULD BE USING TRYCO WAVES IN THAT AREA?

WE SHOULD GET A MORE ACCURATE BEARING FROM THE SATELLITE. IT IS DUE OVER IN TEN MINUTES.

OKAY, FISHER... KEEP ME INFORMED.

RIO DE JANEIRO TO MARINEVILLE...

THE VIDEO SCREEN CLEARS...

WHAT'S ALL THE EXCITEMENT, HARRY?

THAT GIBBERISH WE RECEIVED OVER THE SCRAMBLER. I PUT IT ON THE LANGUAGE TRANSLATOR...

WHAT WAS THE RESULT?

QUICK, FISHER! TURN ON THE SATELLITE CAMERA AT CLOSE RANGE...

SURFACE DWELLERS' MACHINE TO BE DESTROYED AT MAP REF 3720

THAT'S THE ONE, FISHER, HOLD IT THERE... YEAH! JUST AS I THOUGHT... THE NEW MONO-RAIL.

AND THE FIRST TRAIN IS GOING THROUGH TODAY. IT WAS ON TELEVISION. THEY'RE GOING TO BE AMBUSHED... WE'VE GOT TO STOP IT!

AT SPEEDS EXCEEDING 300 MILES AN HOUR THE AMAZON EXPRESS SPEEDS ON...

APPLY MAXIMUM BRAKES!..

STINGRAY

The first Amazon express screams through thick Brazilian jungle at nearly 300 m.p.h. After intercepting a message in an alien tongue and running it through their translation computer, Marineville desperately warns the mono-train of impending disaster . . .

THE BRAKES ARE BURNING UP!

AND SUDDENLY, HALF A MILE DOWN THE TRACK...

ITS BRAKES MELTING, THE EXPRESS COMES TO REST ON THE BRINK OF DISASTER...

THEY *MUST* HOLD OUT . . . THE LINE'S SABOTAGED AHEAD!

YOU OKAY, HAL?

YEAH . . . I THINK SO . . .

COME ON! WE'D BETTER GET THE PASSENGERS OUT BEFORE THE WHOLE LOT GOES UP IN SMOKE.

IN MINUTES THE WRECKED EXPRESS IS EVACUATED FROM THE REAR ESCAPE EXIT...

WHAT ABOUT THAT PLUTONIUM CONSIGNMENT, MR. RYAN?

WE'LL HAVE TO LEAVE IT! THE WHOLE THING'S GOING TO COLLAPSE.

SECONDS LATER...

I SURE HOPE THE WASPS KNOW WHERE WE ARE.

I WOULDN'T MIND BEING STRANDED HERE FOR A YEAR IF I COULD GET MY HANDS ON THE PEOPLE WHO DID THIS!

FAINT RIPPLES DISTURB THE GLASSLIKE SURFACE OF THE LAKE...

... AND TWO THOUSAND FEET DOWN ON THE LAKE BED BELOW...

SO! THE SURFACE DWELLERS' TRANSPORT MACHINE IS DESTROYED, SAFFO.

LET US HOPE THAT NOW THEY WILL GO AWAY FROM OUR LAKE AND LEAVE US IN PEACE!

7

STINGRAY

A U.N. heavy duty helicopter hovers low over an Amazon jungle lake. A terrified message reaches the pilot from the suspended diving chamber which is searching the murky depths for the wreckage of the Pacific-Atlantic Monorail express...

SHE'S GONE, HAL! THE CABLE'S BROKEN!

OKAY, GET THE EMERGENCY CHAMBER READY. I'LL GO DOWN MYSELF.

COME IN U.N. HELICOPTER 374. THIS IS MARINEVILLE.

MAJOR CHESTER, U.N. 374. MAKE IT SNAPPY, MARINEVILLE... I HAVE AN EMERGENCY ON MY HANDS!

THIS IS A SUPERIOR DIRECTIVE, MAJOR! SUSPEND OPERATIONS IMMEDIATELY AND WITHDRAW FROM THE AREA.

BUT I CAN'T DO THAT! ONE OF MY BUDDIES IS TRAPPED AT THE BOTTOM OF THE LAKE!

LISTEN, MAJOR, WITHDRAW IMMEDIATELY! THAT IS AN ORDER!

ATLANTA, ARE TROY AND PHONES HERE?

YES, SIR. THEY'RE RIGHT OUTSIDE.

TROY AND PHONES ARE INTRODUCED TO THE MONORAIL ENGINEER...

IT SURE IS A PLEASURE TO MEET THE CAPTAIN OF STINGRAY.

YOU'RE QUITE A CELEBRITY YOURSELF, MR. RYAN. WE WERE WATCHING YOUR TELEVISION APPEARANCE...

IF THE NICETIES ARE OVER, GENTLEMEN, SHALL WE GET DOWN TO BUSINESS?

THE MARINEVILLE COMMANDER OPERATES A CONTROL...

SOMEWHERE AT THE BOTTOM OF THIS LAKE LIVES AN INTELLIGENT RACE. AND ONE THING WE KNOW ABOUT THEM IS THAT THEY DON'T LIKE THE MONORAIL...

I STILL CAN'T SEE HOW I CAN HELP, COMMANDER.

I WANT YOU TO MODIFY ONE OF YOUR FREIGHT TRAINS TO CARRY STINGRAY TO THE LAKE.

YOU CAN'T BE SERIOUS, COMMANDER!

I'VE NEVER BEEN MORE SERIOUS. CAN YOU TELL ME A QUICKER WAY OF GETTING HER TO THE LAKE?

THE COMMANDER'S RIGHT, TIM... IT WOULD TAKE THE ARMY SEVERAL DAYS TO GET US THERE.

OKAY, BOYS... WE'LL GIVE IT A TRY. BUT IT SURE IS GOING TO TEST THAT MONORAIL'S SUSPENSION STRENGTH.

9

STINGRAY

A new Monotrain express crashes on its maiden voyage across the Brazilian jungle. The Wasps go in to investigate. Commander Shore believes that an alien race living at the bottom of an Amazonian Lake, is responsible for these happenings, and so Stingray is prepared. As a Monorail freighter, carrying Stingray, speeds across land through dense jungle, a reception committee awaits...

COME! THE LAKE GODS HAVE SAID THE WHITE INVADERS WILL BE HERE AT SUN UP. THEY WILL FEEL THE STING OF OUR ARROWS.

MEANWHILE, AT SPEEDS IN EXCESS OF FOUR HUNDRED MILES AN HOUR, THE FREIGHT TRAIN ROCKETS THROUGH THE TROPICAL LANDSCAPE...

I'M JUST OVERHEAD NOW, TROY, IN THE CRANE HELIJET. WE'LL BE AT THE DANGER ZONE IN AN HOUR.

WELL, SO FAR SO GOOD, COMMANDER. THE MONORAIL SEEMS TO BE STANDING UP OKAY. IF THINGS GO ACCORDING TO PLAN WE'LL BE THERE SOON AFTER YOU.

ON BOARD... TROY, PHONES AND TIM RYAN, MONORAIL ENGINEER...

HOW CLOSE WILL WE GO TO THE LAKE, TIM? SURELY THE STRUCTURE CAN'T BE TOO STRONG NEAR THAT WRECKAGE.

IF WE LEAVE A MILE GAP THAT SHOULD BE A GOOD SAFETY MARGIN BY MY ESTIMATION, PHONES.

A RADIO MESSAGE IS RECEIVED...

DAWN BREAKS AS THE HELIJET SURGES FORWARD HIGH ABOVE THE MONORAIL...

SOON THE POWERFUL MOTORS ECHO OVER THE LAKE...

THAT CLEARING RYAN MAPPED OUT... SHOULD BE CLOSE...

THERE IT IS OVER THERE, COMMANDER...

IT ALL LOOKS PEACEFUL ENOUGH... BETTER CHECK THE LIFTING GEAR. WE DON'T WANT TO WASTE TIME WHEN STINGRAY GETS HERE.

RIGHT, SIR...

WHAT THE...

THE HELIJET PILOT SLIDES BACK HIS DOOR HATCH, AND...

STINGRAY

A monorail train has been sabotaged. Commander Shore believes that an alien race living at the bottom of an Amazonian lake is responsible. Stingray is taken overland through the Brazilian jungle by monorail freighter. Troy and Phones reach the lake and dive to investigate, but as they descend through the murky depths they are caught up in a whirlpool...

HOLD TIGHT, PHONES. I'M GOING TO USE MAXIMUM REVS... ACCELERATION RATE SIX.

BUT ACCORDING TO THE MONORAIL COMPANY'S DEPTH SOUNDING ON THIS LAKE IT'S ONLY A THOUSAND FEET AT THE DEEPEST POINT.

RADIO THE COMMANDER AND GET A CORRECT READING. THEY MUST BE TRACKING US.

SUDDENLY, AS QUICKLY AS IT BEGAN, THE WATER TURBULENCE CEASES...

GET THOSE TUBE LIGHTS ON, PHONES. IT'S AS BLACK AS NIGHT OUT THERE.

ON THE SURFACE ABOVE, IN THE MONORAIL FREIGHT TRAIN HEADQUARTERS OF COMMANDER SHORE...

I CAN'T UNDERSTAND IT, SIR... I'M RECEIVING A SIGNAL ON STINGRAY'S WAVELENGTH...BUT ALL I'M GETTING IS THIS HIGH PITCHED BUBBLING.

TRY TO RAISE THEM. SEE WHAT'S GOING ON DOWN THERE.

WE'D BETTER CHECK THE INSTRUMENTS AFTER THAT BATTERING... WHAT'S THE DEPTH READING?

I DON'T BELIEVE IT... SIXTY THOUSAND FEET!

STINGRAY! COME IN PLEASE...

ABOARD STINGRAY...

THAT NOISE! WHAT IN THE NAME OF THUNDER'S GOING ON?

IT'S THE RADIO... THAT'S GONE MAD, TOO.

THE RADIO IS DISCONNECTED... AND SILENCE RETURNS.

PHEW! JUST LISTEN TO THAT QUIET. I'M BEGINNING TO FEEL LIKE ALICE IN WONDERLAND.

13

STINGRAY

Investigating an underwater race believed to have caused a monorail crash, Stingray has dived to the depths of an Amazon lake. But somehow, incredibly, Stingray has been reduced in size . . . and is now at the mercy of a shoal of gigantic piranha . . .

IT'S NO USE, TROY... WE'RE NOT SHAKING THEM OFF...

THERE'S A COUPLE GOING TO ATTACK. HANG ON!

NEEDLE TOOTHED JAWS SNAP SHUT...

I HOPE THESE FELLAS DON'T FIND STINGRAY TOO TASTY...COS THEY SURE LOOK HUNGRY.

WE'LL HAVE TO USE MISSILES, TROY - IT'S THAT OR BE EATEN ALIVE !

ACCELERATION RATE SIX !

FIRE STING MISSILES ONE AND TWO...

HOW'S THAT FOR SHOOTING, TROY ?

PRETTY GOOD, PHONES... NOW LET'S GET OUTTA HERE WHILE THE REST EAT UP THEIR DEAD.

SOON A HEALTHY DISTANCE SEPARATES STINGRAY FROM THE SCAVENGING PIRANHA...

WHAT NOW, TROY ? IN OUR PRESENT REDUCED SIZE WE AREN'T GOING TO POSE MUCH OF A PROBLEM TO WHATEVER WE'RE LOOKING FOR DOWN HERE...

THAT'S A CHANCE WE'VE GOT TO TAKE !

STINGRAY

Following a monorail disaster in the Brazilian jungle, Stingray dives to investigate Commander Shore's theory that aliens living on the bottom of the Amadan lake are to blame. The super sub is caught up in a whirlpool and decreases in size, but a search reveals a sunken city. As they investigate, Troy and Phones are being watched by Amadan scientists . . .

FREEZE THEM AND THEN BRING THEM UP. I WILL TALK TO THEM BEFORE WE CONDUCT THE EXPERIMENT!

VERY WELL, BOSE!

UNAWARE OF THE AMADAN OBSERVATION, TROY AND PHONES WANDER ALONG A VAST DESERTED CORRIDOR, WHEN SUDDENLY...

AAGH! I CAN'T MOVE!

MUST BE THIS GREEN LIGHT!

THE AQUANAUTS FLOAT WEIGHTLESSLY UP TO THE SOURCE OF THE GREEN LIGHT...

THEN A ROOM SEEMS TO MATERIALISE AROUND THEM...

WHAT IS THIS? WHY HAVE WE BEEN BROUGHT HERE?

I'LL TELL YOU!

THE JUNGLE CLEARING WORK ON YOUR MONORAIL HAS WEAKENED THE FOUNDATIONS OF OUR CITY. AT ANY TIME NOW THE WHOLE STRUCTURE WILL COLLAPSE!

WE HAVE EVACUATED OUR CITY, AND THE PEOPLE NOW WAIT IN NEARBY CAVES FOR THE OUTCOME OF THIS EXPERIMENT!

WHEN YOU ENTERED THIS LAKE, YOU AND YOUR CRAFT WERE REDUCED TO AN EIGHTH OF YOUR SURFACE SIZE!

AND NOW WE HOPE TO IMPROVE ON THAT. IF WE ARE SUCCESSFUL WE CAN REDUCE OUR WHOLE RACE TO A SIZE UNDETECTABLE TO THE NAKED EYE!

YOU COULD HAVE MADE YOURSELF KNOWN, AND ASKED FOR OUR HELP!

WE KNOW YOU SURFACE DWELLERS AND YOUR HISTORY OF WAR. WE ARE A PEACEFUL NATION!

EXPERIMENT? WHAT EXPERIMENT?

17

STINGRAY

While investigating the Amadans—a race of people inhabiting a South American deep water lake, Troy and Phones are captured and subjected to a miniaturising experiment. The two aquanauts search for an escape from their test chamber prison . . .

MICROSCOPIC FIGURES, THEY BEGIN THE MUSCLE-BREAKING JOURNEY UPWARDS TO THE ROOF OF THE CHAMBER WHILE OUTSIDE, THE AMADAN SCIENTISTS LIE UNCONSCIOUS AMIDST THE DEBRIS OF THEIR RUINED LABORATORY...

I HOPE YOU'RE RIGHT, TROY...AND THERE IS SOME SORT OF VENTILATION ESCAPE HOLE UP THERE...

SAVE YOUR BREATH, PHONES...WE'VE GOT QUITE A WAY TO GO!

ONLY THE SUPERB PHYSICAL CONDITION OF THE AQUANAUTS ALLOWS THEM TO MAKE THE LAST DESPERATE INCHES...

PHEW! THAT WAS SOME CLIMB!

OUR NEXT PROBLEM IS TO FIND THAT RAY CONTROL PANEL AND SEE IF IT'S STILL OPERATING...

LUCKY THIS GIRDER FELL HERE... IF WE DO MANAGE TO GET THE RAY GOING WE'VE STILL GOT TO GET BACK INTO THE CHAMBER.

LOOKS LIKE THE OTHER END'S LYING ON THE CONTROL PANEL ITSELF.

THESE ARE THE BUTTONS THAT WORK THE THING...BUT THERE'S ONLY ONE WAY TO FIND OUT WHICH IS WHICH...

TROY BRINGS DOWN ALL HIS WEIGHT ONTO THE NEAREST BUTTON...

SO THE OTHER BUTTON MUST BE THE REDUCE OR INCREASE CONTROL. BUT HOW ARE WE GONNA FIND OUT, TROY?

WE DON'T HAVE MUCH CHOICE...

I'M GOING BACK INTO THE TEST CHAMBER. THEN YOU'RE GOING TO BANG THAT CONTROL. I'LL EITHER DISAPPEAR AMONGST THE MICROBES OR COME BACK AND DO THE SAME FOR YOU.

MINUTES LATER TROY SLIDES SAFELY TO THE TEST CHAMBER FLOOR... AND WAITS...

WELL, THIS IS IT... THE MOMENT OF FATE!

FROM HIS POSITION ON THE CONTROL PANEL, PHONES HOLDS HIS BREATH...

IT'S WORKING!

THE END 19

MARINEVILLE CALLING BATTLE STATIONS

Washington H.Q.

Hello, this is Troy Tempest speaking. I've been given the job of showing you around Marineville. This is such an interesting place I'm going to enjoy taking you on a conducted tour. First I think I'd better explain something of the background of our service.

With its headquarters in a magnificent skyscraper in Washington DC, the World Aquanaut Security Patrol is an international organisation with its own surface vessels, submarines, aircraft and rocket bases. The Security Patrol service is designed to protect the world and keep it peaceful.

The W.A.S.P., that is to say the World Aquanaut Security Patrol, is the section of the organisation to which I and my colleagues belong.

Marineville is our base and for security reasons its exact location must remain top secret, but I can tell you, if you promise to keep it to yourself, that it is somewhere on the Pacific Coast of North America.

Now to Marineville itself. The best place to start is the Main Control Room situated within the great tower on top of the central building. This is the hub of all WASP activity...from here the orders are given and operations are planned.

Commander Shore is in charge of Marineville and he is usually to be found in the Main Control Room, gliding about in his motorised chair, directing all ventures and actions in his brusque and efficient manner...and boy, does he keep us on our toes!

Atlanta and Lieutenant Fisher help the Commander to operate the many and compli-

cated control panels and computers built into the Control Room, and a constant watch is maintained on all the seaways of the world in case of trouble.
 Next to the Control Room is the Standby Lounge. When we're on duty, awaiting a mission, this is where Phones, Marina and I relax...until the drumbeat sounds out for action stations. Then we cross to the injector tubes and take up positions in our specially prepared injector seats.

s soon as the drumbeat changes to Launch Stations, we press buttons on our injector seats and are taken down the tubes directly into the cabin of Stingray.

Marineville at Battle Stations

The vessel itself is housed in the Stingray Pen and rests on a launch platform above the water. When we get the "clear to go" order from Atlanta, we operate control and the launch platform goes down, taking Stingray beneath the waves.

Then we are off, heading along the tunnel which leads to the sea and the ocean door. Our progress along the submerged tunnel is followed on a large control panel by Atlanta in the Control Tower.

Because of the vast number of people who work and live at Marineville we have to have living quarters. These are pleasant and modern apartments and houses built around the Control Tower.

Marineville has a hospital, a theatre, shops, stores and everything you would expect to find in a large town, but this town is different because it is a classified area.

This means that no one can enter Marineville without authority from Headquarters. Check points are built at all Marineville entrances and WASP personnel guard these control gates twenty-four hours a day.

With its own fire-station, ambulance bay and power plant, Marineville is completely self-contained. No matter what the situation with the rest of the world, our township can continue to operate.

We have our own airfield where many strike and search aircraft are kept at constant alert, ready for any emergency. These aircraft are the very latest hypersonic vertical take-off machines and travel at fantastic speed.

Adding to the defences of Marineville are the rocket missile bases placed at carefully chosen positions around the complex. The missiles are installed underground, but when the alarm is sounded, the launchers swing up into position and the great remote controlled hydromic and interceptor rockets shoot up to rest automatically on the launch pads, ready for the firing button to be pressed.

A constant radar and laser beam sweep is emitted from the tracking stations on the outskirts of Marineville and these devices warn of any approaching danger to the WASP base.

If the danger is real and urgent then Battle Stations is sounded. The rhythmic, racing drumbeat sounds out and klaxon horns warn all personnel to stand by. Then Commander Shore orders all vehicles to proceed to the nearest ramp area.

The power plant awaits the command from Atlanta to commence Battle Stations procedure. Then Marineville submerges in three stages to its underground position. First the Control Tower and standby rooms go down on the great hydraulic supports. Secondly the living quarters descend and finally the military installations submerge.

As soon as the last building reaches its deep base, Commander Shore gives the order to seal off Marineville. At this stage the heavy steel doors on the surface close completely, hiding and protecting Marineville from the outside world.

Beneath the ground, with the sealed steel doors insuring against attack by any enemy, Marineville can continue to function normally and efficiently.

So this is Marineville. To those who are based here, the installation is more than a vital part of the world's defence system, it is home, a place where serious work and happy entertainment go side by side.

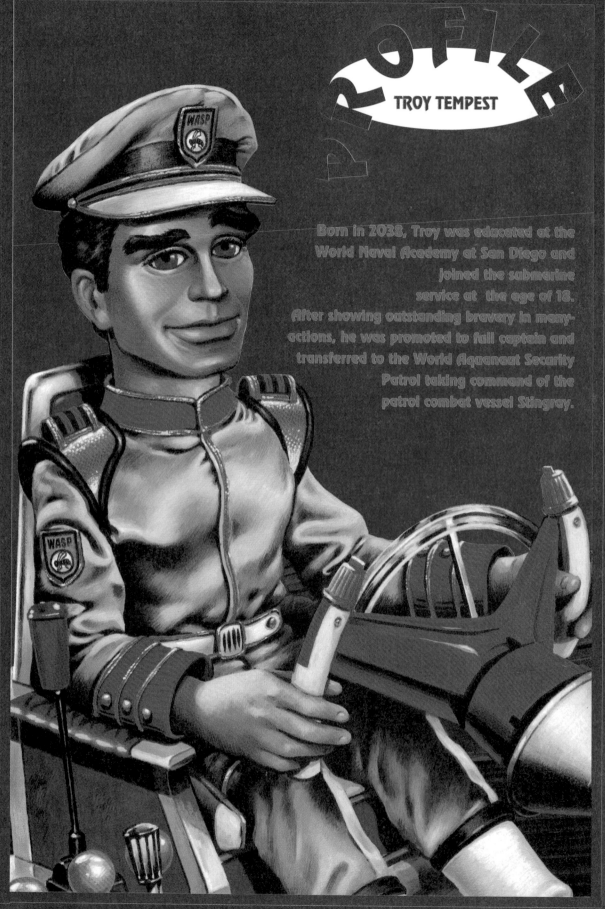

TROY TEMPEST

Born in 2038, Troy was educated at the World Naval Academy at San Diego and joined the submarine service at the age of 18. After showing outstanding bravery in many actions, he was promoted to full captain and transferred to the World Aquanaut Security Patrol taking command of the patrol combat vessel Stingray.

PROFILE

PHONES

PROFILE

MARINA

Beautiful girl from the sea, Marina is the daughter of Aphony and was born 19 marine years ago in the underwater city of Pacifica. She was kidnapped and enslaved by the evil Titan until Troy Tempest helped her to escape from a Terror Fish. Since then she has been a regular Stingray crew member. Although unwilling to speak, Marina's powers of thought telepathy and extra sensory perception make her an invaluable asset to the WASPS.

STINGRAY

In the Marineville tower, Captain Troy Tempest gets his final briefing on an unusual assignment . . .

WELL, THERE IT IS, TROY... IT WON'T BE VERY EXCITING, BUT I CAN ASSURE YOU IT IS A VERY IMPORTANT MISSION.

JUST ABOUT EVERY COUNTRY IS SENDING A REPRESENTATIVE TO THIS THOUSANDTH ANNIVERSARY CELEBRATION OF THE BATTLE OF HASTINGS.

INCLUDING BEREZNIK, COMMANDER ?

YES, SO BE CAREFUL... WE DON'T WANT STINGRAY'S SECRETS FALLING INTO THE WRONG HANDS !

WE'LL KEEP ON THE ALERT, SIR.

His briefing over, Troy joins Phones...

YOU'RE NOT SERIOUS, TROY ? DECKED OUT LIKE SOME CHEAP PLEASURE BOAT AT THIS WATER CARNIVAL...

YOU HEARD WHAT I SAID... NOW COME ON - ORDERS ARE ORDERS.

LAUNCH STATIONS ARE SOUNDED...

ALL ABOARD FOR THE SKYLARK ! TRIPS AROUND THE BAY AT A NICKEL A TIME !

QUIT THAT, PHONES... I'M NO MORE LOOKING FORWARD TO THIS THAN YOU ARE.

As the Stingray crew wait patiently for their passengers, a strange craft approaches the undersea city of Titanica...

WHEN ARE WE MOVING OUT, TROY ?

AS SOON AS OUR PASSENGERS COME ABOARD...

PASSENGERS..?

YEAH... I'M AFRAID THE COMMANDER'S AGREED WE SHOULD TAKE A WORLD TV CAMERA UNIT TO COVER THE PROCEEDINGS.

27

STINGRAY

Stingray speeds from the ocean door, destination England. The Supersub is the Wasp's representative at the 1000th anniversary celebration of the Norman invasion at Hastings. Stingray also carries passengers. A world TV camera team is covering the historic occasion . . .

STINGRAY SEABORNE, COMMANDER.

THAT WILL MAKE YOUR ARRIVAL AT THE ROSARIO TUNNEL 1530 HOURS.

OKAY, PHONES... ACCELERATION RATE SIX. I'D BETTER GO AND GET THIS TV MOB SORTED OUT.

WE SURE DO APOLOGIZE FOR MAKING YOU LATE, CAPTAIN...

THE NAME'S TROY. I GUESS WE'D BETTER FORGET THE WAY WE STARTED. FOR THE NEXT COUPLA WEEKS WE'RE GOING TO BE MIGHTY CLOSE COMPANY.

I'D LIKE TO REMIND YOU GUYS THAT STINGRAY IS A SECURITY VESSEL, SO I MUST ASK YOU ALL TO KEEP ON THIS DECK AND NOT GO WANDERING AROUND.

THESE ARE YOUR CABINS. IF YOU WANT ANYTHING JUST ASK MARINA HERE.

THANKS, TROY...WE'RE GOING TO GET OUR PROGRAMME MATERIAL AND GEAR SORTED OUT.

STINGRAY SPEEDS SOUTH FOLLOWING THE MEXICAN COASTLINE...

WE'VE DONE PRETTY WELL TROY...WE'RE ONLY TEN MINUTES BEHIND OUR ORIGINAL SCHEDULE.

GOOD. BETTER RADIO AHEAD AND GET CLEARANCE FROM THE TUNNEL PEOPLE.

AT ROSARIO TUNNEL CONTROL...

CLEARANCE GRANTED, STINGRAY.

THANKS, WE'LL BE AT ENTRANCE IN APPROXIMATELY SIX MINUTES.

29

STINGRAY

As Stingray speeds through the Rosario tunnel the lights fail and Troy is clubbed unconscious. But Phones manages to save the supersub from colliding with a passing tanker. The TV crew broadcasting from aboard Stingray insinuate that Tempest only fainted . . .

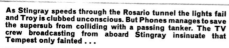

WITH THIS REAL LIFE DRAMA AND THE GOOD NEWS THAT CAPTAIN TEMPEST IS RECOVERING, WE END THIS FIRST BROADCAST FROM WASP SUBMARINE, STINGRAY.

OOOH... MY HEAD!

WHAT HAPPENED, TROY?

YOUR CAPTAIN GOT A TRIFLE PANICKY AND BLACKED OUT.

YEAH... THAT'S HOW IT LOOKED TO ME.

I GUESS WE ALL OWE YOU A BIG THANK-YOU FOR YOUR QUICK ACTION, PHONES... IT COULD HAVE BEEN A NASTY COLLISION.

AS TROY FIGHTS DESPERATELY TO CLEAR HIS MIND STINGRAY EMERGES FROM THE TUNNEL INTO THE CARIBBEAN...

I'M BEGINNING TO REMEMBER. SOMEONE SLUGGED ME.

BUT THAT'S RIDICULOUS. NO-ONE WAS NEAR YOU. YOU MUST HAVE BANGED YOUR HEAD WHEN YOU PASSED OUT.

MR. CASS, WOULD YOU AND YOUR MEN MIND CLEARING THE CONTROL DECK, PLEASE.

THE TV CREW LEAVE...

HAVE I YOUR PERMISSION TO SURFACE, TROY? RECKON WE CAN ALL DO WITH SOME FRESH AIR.

YEAH... TAKE HER UP. LOOK AT THAT, MARINA, THAT'S WHY THE CABIN LIGHTS FAILED.

WHY SHOULD A CABLE SUDDENLY BURN IN TWO LIKE THAT?

STINGRAY REACHES THE SURFACE...

WHY SHOULD SOMEONE TAMPER WITH THE LIGHT CABLE THEN SLUG YOU, TROY?

I DON'T KNOW, PHONES... BUT I SURE INTEND TO FIND OUT.

MARINEVILLE TO STINGRAY...

WHAT IN THUNDER IS GOING ON, TEMPEST? I'VE JUST SEEN THAT TV REPORT AND IT DIDN'T DO THE WASP IMAGE ANY GOOD AT ALL.

I'M MAKING CERTAIN INVESTIGATIONS, COMMANDER. I'LL GIVE YOU A REPORT SOON.

STINGRAY

Stingray is on her way to England for the celebration of the Hastings invasion when strange things begin to happen. The ship is plunged into darkness and almost collides with a passing tanker. Then a Sting-missile breaks loose from its mounting . . .

MARINA — LOOK OUT!

DANGER IS AVERTED JUST IN TIME . . .

OUCH, MY ARM . . . ARE YOU OKAY, MARINA?

MARINA! PHONES . . . WHAT HAPPENED?

HOW DID THAT GET DOWN THERE?

I DON'T KNOW, TROY. WOULD YOU MIND GIVING ME A HAND? I'VE WRENCHED MY SHOULDER.

I TOLD YOU TV GUYS THAT YOU WEREN'T ALLOWED HERE!

GEE . . . THAT MISSILE ON THE DECK . . . IT COULD'VE BLOWN US ALL TO SMITHEREENS IF IT EXPLODED.

I'M NOT TELLING YOU PEOPLE AGAIN . . . GET BACK TO YOUR CABINS!

THE TWO MEN OBEY . . .

WHAT'S ALL THE COMMOTION?

WE NEARLY GOT BLOWN SKY HIGH, THAT'S ALL . . .

IF THIS IS THE W.A.S.P.S THANK HEAVENS FOR THE WORLD NAVY.

WHILE MARINA ADMINISTERS FIRST AID, TROY DOES A SPOT OF INVESTIGATING . . .

SOMEONE'S DELIBERATELY TAMPERED WITH THESE LOCKING CHAINS . . .

THAT DOESN'T SURPRISE ME . . . I SAW SOMEBODY IN THE SHADOW PUSHING THAT MISSILE OFF THE RACK.

THE MISSILE IS REPLACED AND NEW LOCKING CHAINS ARE FITTED TO HOLD IT IN POSITION...

IT'S A GOOD JOB THOSE STING-MISSILE WARHEADS AREN'T PRIMED UNTIL THEY ENTER THE LAUNCH TUBES, TROY.

YEAH... WHAT BOTHERS ME NOW, PHONES, IS WITH FOUR THOUSAND MILES TO GO BEFORE WE REACH ENGLAND WHAT'S OUR ENEMY'S NEXT MOVE GOING TO BE?

UNKNOWN TO TROY, TITAN'S AGENT BARRACUDA IS ALREADY MAKING HIS PLANS...

MY NEXT MOVE WILL SEPARATE TEMPEST FROM HIS CREW, X20.

MIGHTY TITAN WILL REWARD YOU WELL FOR THIS.

WITH WORK COMPLETED IN THE MISSILE ROOM THE STINGRAY CREW RETURN TO CONTROL CENTRE...

YOU TWO MUST STILL BE SHAKEN UP, SO TURN IN. I'VE GOTTA MAKE MY REPORT TO MARINEVILLE, SO I MIGHT AS WELL FINISH THE NIGHT'S WATCH.

THANKS, TROY.

STINGRAY

MINUTES LATER, TROY SITS AT THE TRANSMITTER TO MAKE HIS REPORT...

THAT SHOULD DO IT... WHO'S?

WHAT THE? AAGH!

SLEEP TIGHT, CAPTAIN TEMPEST.

YELLOW CHANNEL OPEN, STING...

SORRY, MARINEVILLE THERE'S BEEN A SLIGHT TECHNICAL SNAG.

LOOKS AS IF YOUR PRECIOUS CAPTAIN WAS FRIGHTENED WE'D REPORT THAT MISSILE INCIDENT, DOESN'T LOOK AS IF HE WAS TOO KEEN ON PASSING IT ON HIMSELF, EITHER...

TROY...?

NEXT MORNING, PHONES GETS A RUDE AWAKENING...

ALL RIGHT, ALL RIGHT, THERE'S NO NEED TO BUST THE DOOR.

LIEUTENANT SHERIDAN, SOMEONE HAS DELIBERATELY DESTROYED OUR EQUIPMENT...

HAVE YOU REPORTED IT TO TROY.

THAT'S A JOKE... YOU'D BETTER COME WITH US.

33

STINGRAY

Stingray is on her way to England to take part in the Battle of Hastings celebrations. The sub's radio and the equipment of the TV crew aboard are mysteriously wrecked . . . and the wrecker fixes it to look as though Troy Tempest is responsible . . .

HE'S GONE NUTS! HE MUST HAVE HAD SOME SORT OF A BREAKDOWN!

STOP SURMISING AND HELP ME GET HIM TO HIS CABIN!

WITH NO CAPTAIN AND AN INJURY TO YOURSELF, WHAT DO YOU PLAN ON DOING?

I'M TAKING OVER. WHATEVER HAPPENS THE W.A.S.P.S ARE GOING TO BE REPRESENTED IN ENGLAND.

HOW ABOUT SOME ASSISTANCE FROM YOUR MAINTENANCE GUY IN REBUILDING THE RADIO, MR. CASS?

MINUTES LATER, TROY AWAKENS FROM A TROUBLED SLEEP...

WHAT A STRANGE DREAM...A GUY IN A GASMASK...PUMPING GAS AT ME...WHAT'S THE TIME...EIGHT THIRTY!

THE DOOR'S LOCKED. WHAT IN THUNDER'S GOING ON ROUND HERE? LET ME OUT!

TROY CREATES SUCH A DIN IT SOON ATTRACTS NOTICE...

STAND AWAY FROM THE DOOR, TROY... I'VE GOT A GUN AND IF NECESSARY I'LL USE IT.

SORRY, TROY... BUT I'VE HAD TO TAKE OVER COMMAND.

YOU'VE MADE A BIG MISTAKE, LIEUTENANT. I'LL SEE YOU'RE COURT-MARTIALLED FOR THIS.

PHONES AND MARINA LEAVE...

ONE OF THOSE TV GUYS IS TRYING TO DESTROY ME AND STINGRAY, AND HE'S DOING A PRETTY GOOD JOB!...EVEN PHONES AND MARINA ARE ON HIS SIDE.

STINGRAY

Titan has hired the Hood to cause havoc aboard Stingray where he has been masquerading as a World TV Commentator. With Troy imprisoned in his cabin, the Hood now comes into the open and orders Phones to destroy the World's finest fighting ships which are assembled in the English channel to take part in the millennium celebrations of the Battle of Hastings . . .

ONE FALSE MOVE AND YOU ALL DIE. NOW, LIEUTENANT, SHALL WE DIVE AND BEGIN THE ATTACK?

YOU MUST BE MAD . . . IT'LL START A WORLD WAR!

LET'S NOT BE SQUEAMISH, LIEUTENANT . . . THAT IS NO CONCERN OF MINE!

SUDDENLY . . .

AAAGH!

GUESS MY ARM DON'T FEEL SO BAD AFTER ALL! YOU MADE A BIG MISTAKE THINKING YOU COULD SPLIT A WASP CREW, MISTER.

YOU FREE TROY, MARINA, WHILE I GET OUR FRIEND SAFELY TUCKED AWAY.

SOON A FULL REPORT IS MADE TO MARINEVILLE . . .

SO YOU THINK IT'S THE HOOD, EH, TROY? YOU'D BETTER SEND DETAILS AND I'LL CHECK IT OUT WITH SECURITY.

I'LL SWITCH ON THE CAMERAS AND YOU CAN TAKE A LOOK FOR YOURSELF, SIR.

SECRET CAMERAS CONCEALED IN STINGRAY'S CONFINEMENT CELL BEGIN TO OPERATE . . .

IT IS TIME MY LITTLE WATER-DWELLING FRIEND LEARNT OF MY PREDICAMENT.

AND . . .

SIGNALS FROM THE HOOD'S SHOE TRANSMITTER REACH THEIR DESTINATION...

WHAT IS THIS? BARRACUDA'S EMERGENCY WARNING...

SO HE HAS FAILED. MIGHTY TITAN WILL NOT BE PLEASED...BUT IF HE WAS TO ESCAPE, HE WOULD ACT AS USEFUL BAIT TO DESTROY STINGRAY. I MUST PLAN CAREFULLY.

MEANWHILE, COMMANDER SHORE CONFIRMS THE HOOD'S IDENTITY AND GIVES TROY NEW ORDERS...

HE'S WANTED BY JUST ABOUT EVERY COUNTRY IN THE WORLD. AS YOU'RE INSIDE BRITISH TERRITORIAL WATERS I'M AFRAID YOU'LL HAVE TO HAND HIM OVER.

AFTER WHAT HE TRIED TO DO TO US AND STINGRAY?

I KNOW HOW YOU FEEL, TROY. BUT THAT'S WORLD GOVERNMENT LAW. I'VE REQUESTED THOSE TV GUYS ARE TAKEN OFF AT THE SAME TIME.

OKAY COMMANDER, YOU'RE THE BOSS.

MINUTES LATER...

HERE'S THE POLICE-LAUNCH, TROY...

RIGHT, PHONES... BRING THE PRISONER UP AND TELL THOSE TV BOYS TO BE READY.

STINGRA

IF YOU'LL JUST SIGN THIS WARRANT, CAPTAIN, WE'LL BE ON OUR WAY.

TAKE GOOD CARE OF HIM, SERGEANT... HE CAUSED US A PILE OF TROUBLE.

NO HARD FEELINGS, TROY... IT MUST HAVE LOOKED AS IF WE HAD A HAND IN THINGS TOO...

FORGET IT... WASP PERSONNEL DON'T BEAR GRUDGES. NICE TO HAVE MET YOU.

POLICE

THE POLICE-LAUNCH HEADS TOWARDS LAND AND ROUNDS A SMALL ROCKY PROMONTORY... THEN, SUDDENLY...

WELL, I FOR ONE AIN'T SORRY TO SEE THEM GO.

YEAH... I SUPPOSE WE'D BETTER REPORT TO THE CELEBRATION ORGANISER.

POLICE

LOOK OUT!

POLICE

After planning to take over Stingray and then destroy the International fleet which is anchored in the English channel, the Hood is captured and handed over to the British Police. As their launch ploughs landward . . .

QUICKLY : CATCH THE LINE... WE HAVE NO TIME TO WASTE.

WE MUST FIND SOMEWHERE TO HIDE... SOON THESE WATERS WILL BE ALIVE WITH BRITISH POLICE.

REMOVE THESE HANDCUFFS.

NO, MY FRIEND... YOU HAVE FAILED IN YOUR TASK, AND TITAN IS ANGRY.

NOW YOU MUST PAY THE PRICE OF FAILURE.... IF MY PLAN IS SUCCESSFUL I WILL KILL TEMPEST, BUT UNFORTUNATELY YOU TOO WILL HAVE TO DIE.

TROY ASKS FOR A DESCRIPTION OF THE SUB...

THERE'S ONLY ONE CRAFT I KNOW THAT FITS THAT DESCRIPTION-X20'S!

STINGRAY'S CAPTAIN HEARS OF THE HOOD'S ESCAPE...

SORRY, CAPTAIN...WE'VE PICKED UP THE OTHER FOUR BUT THE PRISONER ESCAPED...

YOU SAY HE WENT ABOARD THIS STRANGE SUB ?

YEAH, THAT COULD ACCOUNT FOR A LOT OF THINGS. THANKS INSPECTOR.

WE RECKON THEY'RE OUT OF OUR TERRITORIAL WATERS BY NOW. THE WORLD POLICE HAVE BEEN ALERTED.

STINGRAY

Unaware of impending danger, Troy and Phones search for Titan's agent X20 and the Hood, his ally in a recent attempt to destroy Stingray . . .

WELL, WELL...NOW HOW DID YOU GET DOWN THERE?

AND WHERE'S YOUR FRIEND?

OUTSIDE, ON THE MISTY CLIFF PATH...

MY MOMENT OF TRIUMPH! DIE, TROY TEMPEST, DIE!

TEMPEST WILL BOTHER US NO MORE, MIGHTY TITAN.

EXCELLENT! RETURN TO TITANICA IMMEDIATELY. WE MUST MAKE NEW PLANS TO BEGIN OUR ALL-OUT WAR AGAINST THE TERRAINEAN'S.

DEEP IN THE CLIFF THE DUST BEGINS TO SETTLE...

COUGH...COUGH...ARE YOU OKAY, PHONES?

YEAH...I...I...THINK SO, TROY.

TAKE THOSE BRACELETS OFF OUR FRIEND. IF WE'RE ALL GOING TO DIE THERE'S NO REASON WHY HE SHOULD BE TRUSSED UP LIKE A TURKEY.

WE'RE NOT DEAD YET, CAPTAIN.

WHAT D'YOU MEAN?

DON'T YOU NOTICE THAT ALTHOUGH THIS CHAMBER IS NOW SEALED, THE AIR IS STILL FRESH?

SAY, TROY...HE'S RIGHT!

PROFILE

TITAN

PROFILE

X2 ZERO

Two hundred and thirty marine years old, Titan is undisputed King of the undersea city of Titanica. He has sworn to take over the terrain and wages a perpetual war against Marineville. His subjects, the Aquaphibians, bow down to his ruthless bidding and live in fear of his changing moods and cold-blooded, evil schemes.

Creeping, meanly mouthed toady of Titan, X2 Zero is a surface agent for Titanica operating from his secret hideout - an old house on the Isle of Lemoy. Born in a city which was many years ago conquered by Titan, X2 Zero is 107 marine years old. The house of Lemoy contains many complex computers and control systems which can be hidden at the touch of a button.

PROFILE

ATLANTA

Made a lieutenant after six years of intensive control tuition, Atlanta is the daughter of Commander Shore. Born in California, the 23-year-old auburn-haired Atlanta had many extra problems laid at her door when her mother died seven years ago. She had to take over the domestic duties in the Shore household in between her control shifts at Marineville's Tower.

Christened Samuel Arthur, Commander Shore was born in Kansas in 2015. He ran away to sea at an early age and after joining the navy gained rapid promotion. Tragedy struck the Commander some years ago when his submarine was attacked by an undersea alien. His injuries from this engagement confined him to a motorised hover chair and he was given the great task of commanding WASP HQ at Marineville.

PROFILE

COMMANDER SHORE

SPECIFICATIONS OF
STINGRAY

1
2
3
7
8
5
4
6
22

1. Starboard hydroplane. 2. Ratemaster assembly: featuring a contra-rotating anti-torque eddy damper. 3. Atomic generator, feeding twin motors driving the Drumman-WASP hydrojet. 4. Airlock access to starboard Aquasprite, a two-man mini-submarine. 5. Aft trim tanks. 6. Starboard heat disipator and midships tanks. 7. Topside emergency exit hatch. 8. Standby lounge with navigation computer and library. 9. Periscope, featuring zoom lens video-scan recording system. 10. Conning tower hatch, through which ejector launch tubes from the Stingray pen pass. 11. Periscope arm swings clear when hatch in use. 12. Lower deck wardroom, with galley, sleeping quarters and maintenance areas to the rear (for main engine) and forward (to equipment bays and auxiliary engine). 13. Main control cabin, with cahelium-strengthened all-round window for maximum visibility. 14. Main computer monitors ship's life support systems, including cabin temperature and pressurisation. 15. Sting missile bay. 16. Auxiliary engine room. 17. Air compression and recycling unit. 18. Pressurised diaphragm air-from-water extractors. 19. Electronics and general maintenance bay. 20. Monocoptor exit hatch. 21. Three monocoptors - each is a personal anti-gravity transport system for crew members travelling between the surfaced Stingray and the nearest shoreline. 22. Starboard stabilising fin with integrated booster unit. 23. Starboard navigation light (retracts when missile is fired). 24. Forward trim tanks. 25. Forward sonar dome.

Stingray is the World Aquanaut Security Patrol's fastest and most up-to-date submarine, achieving a staggering underwater speed of 600 knots. The craft has been in gradual development for 20 years when early versions of the Drumman-WASP hydrojet and Ratemaster propulsion systems were built for the first Stingray test-bed craft in 2064. It is piloted by Captain Troy Tempest and Lee 'Phones' Sheridan. It is expected that a whole fleet of these craft will be built to replace the existing WASP submarine fleet within the next 10 years.

STINGRAY

The WASP's most effective patrol/combat security vessel, this revolutionary undersea craft has a top speed of 600 knots and the power to dive safely to depths never before envisaged by civilian engineering designers. Continually being modified to meet the new demands placed upon it, Stingray has been in service for three years and its success against hostile attackers has been phenomenal.

PROFILE

TERROR FISH

Titan's main line of attack, the Terror Fish, also called the Mechanical Fish, is constructed of fused coral Titanum, an undersea material manufactured to Titan's own formula. It is tremendously strong yet effectively light. Generally manned by two Aquaphibians, a Terror Fish carries many armaments and deadly missiles and is capable of fantastic speeds beneath the water.

STINGRAY

AT SOUTHAMPTON DOCKS, ENGLAND, STINGRAY PREPARES TO RETURN TO MARINEVILLE.

NICE TO HAVE MET YOU, MR. HAVENS.

PLEASURE TO HAVE SUCH FAMOUS VISITORS IN MY HARBOUR, CAPTAIN TEMPEST.

MARINEVILLE ON THE HOT LINE, TROY.

THERE'S A CHANGE OR ORDERS, TROY. TROUBLE IS BREWING AT THE NEW WASP BASE IN SCOTLAND.

THE SCOTLAND LOCH FIONN PROJECT... I THOUGHT ALL THAT WAS GOING THROUGH ON SCHEDULE.

THINGS WERE GOING FINE UNTIL TWO WEEKS AGO... THEN THE SABOTAGE BROKE OUT.

HOW DO WE FIT IN, ATLANTA?

COMMANDER JORDAN IN CHARGE OF THE PROJECT HAS INJURED HIS BACK AFTER A MYSTERIOUS ACCIDENT. YOU'RE HIS REPLACEMENT.

I'M WHAT, ATLANTA? A LAND-BASED JOB!

MINUTES LATER, STINGRAY SAILS FROM SOUTHAMPTON...

GEE, MARINA... FANCY THE COMMANDER BUSTING US UP LIKE THIS. THINGS WON'T BE THE SAME WITHOUT TROY.

SOON, BRITAIN'S CRACK MONORAIL EXPRESS 'BALMORAL BIRD' IS CARRYING TROY THROUGH ENGLAND AND INTO THE SCOTTISH LOWLANDS...

TROY FEELS THE SAME WAY...

EDINBURGH, SINGLE, PLEASE...

AFTER ALL THAT TIME TO BE PARTED FROM STINGRAY... WHAT HURTS MORE IS THAT THE COMMANDER DIDN'T TELL ME HIMSELF.

ANOTHER FIVE MINUTES TO EDINBURGH, CAPTAIN.

THANKS!

GOOD AFTERNOON, SIR. THE NAME'S MACLEOD... IF YOU'LL JUMP IN WE'LL BE OFF TO LOCH FIONN.

OKAY... LET'S GET GOING.

I HEAR YOU'VE BEEN HITTING A FEW SNAGS, LIEUTENANT.

YES, CAPTAIN. IT STARTED FOUR MONTHS AGO WHEN WE BEGAN BLOWING THE OCEAN TUNNEL FROM LOCH EWE TO LOCH FIONN.

48

FIRST A BADGER DRILLING UNIT WENT HAYWIRE...

THEN THE AIR SUPPLY TO THE TUNNEL BECAME CONTAMINATED...

A DAY LATER A MYSTERIOUS CHARGE EXPLODED OVER NIGHT AND FLOODED THE WHOLE TUNNEL.

AND NOW, OF COURSE, THE STATION COMMANDER'S SEA BUG CRASHES.

WASP BASE, LOCH FIONN, IS REACHED...

...AND THESE ARE YOUR QUARTERS. IF YOU'LL BE READY IN AN HOUR I'LL TAKE YOU TO MEET THE LAIRD.

THE WHO?

SHALL I TAKE YOU FOR A TRIP AROUND, CAPTAIN?

I SUPPOSE I MIGHT AS WELL GET THE FEEL OF THE LAYOUT, THANKS.

TRADITION, CAPTAIN. AS THE WASP BASE IS ON HIS LAND IT'S THE CUSTOM FOR US TO FOLLOW LOCAL PROCEDURE.

SO I HAVE TO GO AND PAY MY RESPECTS TO SOME ANCIENT SCOTSMAN, EH?

THAT EVENING...

IS THAT THE LAIRD'S PLACE?

AYE, SIX HUNDRED YEARS OF SCOTTISH HISTORY ARE IN THOSE STONES.

AND SOON...

I'M VERY PLEASED TO MAKE YOUR AQUAINTANCE, SIR... AND NOW I'D LIKE YOU TO MEET MY GUEST.

I THINK YOU TWO HAVE MET.

COMMANDER SHORE!

49

STINGRAY

Troy Tempest arrives in Scotland to take command of the partly completed W.A.S.P. base at Loch Fionn, where mysterious accidents have halted progress. Troy visits the local Laird, and finds Commander Shore present...

YOU MUST BE PRETTY SORE AT ME, TROY, BUT THERE WERE GOOD REASONS FOR DOING THINGS THE WAY I DID.

YOU CAN TELL TROY OVER DINNER, SAM.

WE HAD TO BRING YOU IN THIS WAY: THE NORMAL CHANNELS ARE OPEN TO ALL WASP PERSONNEL.

YOU SEE, TROY, WE'RE CERTAIN OUR SABOTEUR IS A WASP MAN.

MACLEOD'S THE BASE SECURITY OFFICER. HIS JOB HAS BEEN HAMPERED BECAUSE EVEN THE RETIRING COMMANDER WAS UNDER SUSPICION.

HOW DO I FIT INTO THINGS?

OUR SABOTEUR HAS ALREADY GOT RID OF ONE BASE COMMANDER AND WHATEVER HE'S AFTER IS SO IMPORTANT TO HIM HE'LL PROBABLY TRY TO REMOVE YOU TOO, TROY.

WHAT ABOUT STINGRAY, COMMANDER - I SUPPOSE SHE'S RETURNED TO MARINEVILLE?

SHE'S CRUISING TWO MILES OFF SHORE. THIS WAY WE HAVE UNSABOTAGED EQUIPMENT AVAILABLE FOR UNDERWATER WORK IF NECESSARY.

WILL YOU BE STAYING HERE, SIR?

AS AN EX-WASP OFFICER MYSELF, I OFFERED MY HOUSE AS SAM'S HEADQUARTERS.

WHILE TROY AND THE OTHERS MAKE THEIR FINAL PLANS INSIDE THE CASTLE...

THAT SHOULD DO IT. AN EFFICIENT WAY TO KILL TWO BIRDS WITH ONE STONE.

AND A FEW MINUTES LATER...

BE CAREFUL CAPTAIN TEMPEST, WE'RE UP AGAINST A DANGEROUS MAN.

DON'T YOU FRET, SIR, I CAN TAKE CARE OF MYSELF... AND THANKS FOR THE EXCELLENT DINNER.

51

STINGRAY

Troy Tempest and Lieutenant Macleod are returning to the partly constructed W.A.S.P. base at Loch Fionn when their sabotaged car crashes. Troy manages to drag the unconscious Macleod clear before the wreck totters over the edge of a cliff. The Captain then tries to stop a passing car for help, but . . .

AS TROY LIES WAITING FOR THE WOULD-BE ASSASSIN TO RETURN HE PUTS OUT AN EMERGENCY CALL ON HIS WRIST RADIO...

IF I LIE STILL HE MAY COME BACK TO VIEW HIS HANDIWORK...

SHORE SPEAKING... WHAT'S THE BOTHER, TROY?

TROY MAKES HIS REPORT...

PLAY IT CAREFULLY, TROY, AND WE MIGHT HAVE OUR MAN AT LAST.

HE'S PROBABLY TAKING A LOOK AT US THROUGH BLACK-LIGHT GLASSES NOW.

TROY IS CORRECT, FOR AT THAT MOMENT...

LOOKS AS IF I HIT HIM AFTER ALL. BETTER GO BACK AND MAKE SURE.

AND SOON...

HASN'T MOVED... BETTER DUMP HIM AND MACLEOD OVER CLIFF.

SORRY, CAPTAIN TEMPEST, BUT YOU'VE COME BETWEEN ME AND MY PLANS TO TAKE THE McEWAN HOARD.

SORRY, MISTER, BUT I DON'T AIM ON CO-OPERATING

HUH?

I THINK IT'S ABOUT TIME YOU TOLD ME YOUR NAME, FELLA...

OUF!

BUT AS TROY STEPS FORWARD...

AAGH!

THE OTHER MAN TAKES HIS CHANCE...

AAGH!

SORRY, SIR, I LET HIM GET AWAY THIS TIME... BUT HIS DAYS ARE NUMBERED NOW...

WHAT D'YOU MEAN, TROY?

THE DISTANT NOISE OF AN APPROACHING CAR DISTURBS THE NIGHT AIR...

I'D RECOGNISE THAT VOICE ANYWHERE. IT'S JUST A MATTER OF GOING THROUGH THE BASE PERSONNEL UNTIL I FIND HIM.

NEXT MORNING TROY HOLDS AN INFORMAL PARADE OF THE W.A.S.P. STAFF AT LOCH FIONN...

OKAY, LIEUTENANT... WRAP IT UP. DISMISS THE MEN AND GET THEM BACK TO THEIR DUTIES.

YES, SIR.

HE'S CERTAINLY NOT HERE... PERHAPS IT ISN'T A WASP AFTER ALL. I'LL REPORT TO THE COMMANDER THEN GO OVER AND SEE MACLEOD IN THE INFIRMARY.

MACLEOD HAS RECOVERED...

GLAD TO SEE YOU'RE OKAY.

HALLO, JIM... I'VE JUST BEEN TOLD YOU WERE IN HERE. SO OUR BOGEY MAN HAD A GO AT YOU TOO.

CAPTAIN TEMPEST, THIS IS YOUR PREDECESSOR, COMMANDER BARRETT.

PLEASED TO MAKE YOUR ACQUAINTANCE, CAPTAIN, HOPE YOU HAVE BETTER LUCK THAN ME.

YEAH, SO DO I, COMMANDER...

THAT'S HIM... THE SAME VOICE AS THE GUY WHO ATTACKED US LAST NIGHT... I'LL SWEAR IT!

STINGRAY

A mystery saboteur is determined to close the partly constructed W.A.S.P. base at Loch Fionn. The only clue Stingray's captain has of the saboteur is his voice, and now Troy believes he has identified him as ex-base commander Barrett . . .

IT IS MOST INADVISABLE THAT YOU SHOULD BE OUT OF BED WITH THAT LEG, COMMANDER...

SORRY, BOYS, BUT YOU HAVE TO FOLLOW DOCTOR'S ORDERS.

THAT'S OUR MAN, JIM. I'D RECOGNISE THAT VOICE ANYWHERE.

COMMANDER BARRETT! IT HARDLY SEEMS POSSIBLE, TROY. WHAT ON EARTH CAN HE BE AFTER?

DOES THE McEWAN HOARD MEAN ANYTHING TO YOU, JIM?

SO YOU'VE HEARD OUR LOCAL FAIRY TALE, TROY?

LEGEND HAS IT THAT SOME SHIPS OF THE SPANISH ARMADA FLED FROM THE ENGLISH AND FOUNDERED OFF THE COAST NEAR THE ISLE OF EWE...

A LOCAL OUTLAW CHIEF NAMED McEWAN, LOOTED A TREASURE SHIP AND STASHED IT AWAY TO FINANCE HIS FIGHT AGAINST ELIZABETH AND THE ENGLISH.

OUTSIDE MACLEOD'S ROOM...

YOU THINK THIS IS THE ANSWER TO OUR MYSTERY TROY?

YOU'LL HAVE TO BE SILENCED CAPTAIN TEMPEST... AND I THINK I KNOW HOW...

YES I DO. KEEP AN EYE ON HIM WHILE I GO AND MAKE A REPORT.

MINUTES LATER TROY LEAVES THE W.A.S.P. MEDICAL CENTRE...

HALLO... WHAT'S THIS?

your silence = Macleod's life.

55

STINGRAY

Ex-W.A.S.P. Commander Barrett is holding Phones and Jim McLeod hostage in an effort to blackmail Troy into using Stingray to move a hoard of 16th century treasure. Troy agrees but leaves a message with Dr. Savi for Commander Shore, who is a secret guest of the local laird. Unfortunately for Stingray's captain, Savi is in league with Barrett . . .

THERE SHE IS, CAPTAIN.

THAT'S THE PRETTIEST SIGHT I'VE SEEN FOR WEEKS, LIEUTENANT.

TROY IS BACK AT THE CONTROLS...

SURE IS GOOD TO BE BACK...ONLY WISH PHONES WAS HERE TOO...WE'VE GOTTA GET HIM OUT OF THIS MESS.

MEANWHILE, PHONES IS MAKING HIS OWN EFFORTS TO GET FREE...

JIM...IF YOU'RE FEELING OKAY, A FEW TUGS ON THAT LEFT HAND CHAIN MIGHT PRODUCE RESULTS...

ALL RIGHT, WE'LL GIVE IT A GO...

FOR LONG, SKIN-CHAFING MINUTES, MACLEOD EXERTS HIS STRENGTH AGAINST THE EATEN METAL...

IT'S NO GOOD, PHONES, IT'S NOT EVEN BUDGING...

HANG ON... I'LL LEND YOU A HAND...

COME ON, YOU BRUTE... GIVE...

THEN...

IT'S GONE!

WE'LL NEED DIVING GEAR TO GET OUT INTO THE TUNNEL... WHAT'S OUR NEXT MOVE, PHONES?

SURELY THERE MUST BE SOME OTHER WAY INTO THIS CAVE?

INCH BY INCH THE W.A.S.P. MEN COVER THE ROCKY WALLS...

IT'S NO GOOD, PHONES... THE SURFACE TUNNEL THAT McEWAN USED HAS PROBABLY FALLEN IN...

I'M AFRAID YOU'RE RIGHT, JIM... WHAT'S THAT NOISE?

UNKNOWINGLY, JIM HAS TRIGGERED THE ENTRANCE TO A SECRET STAIRCASE...

COME ON, PHONES!

TROY WAITS IMPATIENTLY FOR HIS RENDEZVOUS WITH BARRETT...

WHAT'S BARRETT PLAYING AT NOW? HE WAS SUPPOSED TO MAKE CONTACT TWENTY MINUTES AGO... WHAT IS IT, MARINA?

A SKIN DIVER...THAT MUST BE HIM.

SOON BARRETT IS ABOARD THE SUPERSUB...

MY APOLOGIES FOR KEEPING YOU WAITING, CAPTAIN...BUT I HAD TO MAKE SURE YOU HADN'T PREPARED AN AMBUSH.

THAT WOULD HAVE BEEN MOST UNWISE. YOU SEE I HAVE LEFT AN EXPLOSIVE DEVICE IN THE CAVE WITH YOUR FRIENDS, AND IF I FAIL TO RETURN IN TWENTY MINUTES...

TROY FOLLOWS BARRETT'S ORDERS AND SOON STINGRAY IS ENTERING THE HALF COMPLETED OCEAN TUNNEL...

THIS IS AS FAR AS I CAN GO WITHOUT COLLIDING WITH ONE OF THE CONSTRUCTION MACHINES.

RIGHT. GET INTO DIVING GEAR. WE'VE SOME CARRYING TO DO.

SECONDS LATER, THE EX-W.A.S.P. COMMANDER SURFACES IN THE TREASURE CAVE...

THE PRISONERS— THEY'RE GONE...I HAVE LOOKED EVERYWHERE!

DON'T PANIC... THE TREASURE'S STILL HERE, ISN'T IT? HIDE YOURSELF AWAY. I MIGHT NEED YOUR SERVICES IF TEMPEST WON'T CO-OPERATE...

COME ON, TEMPEST, LET'S GET THESE CHESTS ABOARD STINGRAY.

I'M NOT SHIFTING ANYTHING UNTIL I'VE SEEN PHONES AND MACLEOD! AND THAT'S...

...FINAL! AAGH!

STINGRAY

Renegade W.A.S.P. officers Barrett and Savi, responsible for the sabotage of the Loch Fionn base, move their treasure aboard Stingray. After the final chest is safely stored on the supersub, Savi resurfaces in the underground lake once again, where Troy Tempest is held captive . . .

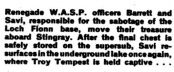

BARRETT! THE GIRL... SHE'S GONE!

PROBABLY ATTEMPTING TO RAISE THE ALARM.

YOU'LL NEVER GET AWAY WITH IT, BARRETT.

BY THE TIME COMMANDER SHORE DISCOVERS WHAT HAS HAPPENED WE SHALL BE WELL ON OUR WAY.

YOU MUST BE MAD, BARRETT. NO COUNTRY UNDER WORLD GOVERNMENT ADMINISTRATION WILL GRANT YOU ASYLUM.

WITH THE EXCEPTION OF ONE...WHICH HAS USED MY SERVICES...

BEREZNIK!

EXACTLY, CAPTAIN TEMPEST. PLEASANT DREAMS.

I'VE GOT TO MAKE AN EFFORT TO GET FREE...WHAT'S THAT NOISE..?

JIM!

NO TIME TO EXPLAIN, TROY. GO UP THE STAIRCASE, IT LEADS TO THE CASTLE, COMMANDER SHORE'S WAITING...I'LL FIX THAT BOMB.

MEANWHILE, BARRETT BOARDS STINGRAY...

THERE'S NO TIME TO WASTE—LET'S GET OUT OF HERE.

GET THAT TREASURE LOADED INTO A SEABUG! THE WASPS WON'T BE FAR BEHIND.

MARINEVILLE CONTROL CENTRE

CONTROL ROOM

Part of the intricate machinery in the Control Room is the video-phone. Connected to WASP HQ in Washington DC the videophone is a television phone link allowing the caller to see as well as hear the person to whom he is speaking. But a control is attached to eliminate vision if required. The Automatic Sea Map, another part of the WASP machinery, is used extensively to track the course of vessels at sea. An electrically controlled Locator Compass is used in pin-pointing the exact bearing of WASP vessels.

TUNNEL SCANNER

The Tunnel Scanner is manned by Atlanta, daughter of Commander Shore, to view craft at the tunnel's ocean entrance and as they pass through its interior. If necessary, Atlanta can refuse entry to craft which arouse suspicion. At the press of a button she can raise or close the huge door which seals the entrance.

STANDBY LOUNGE

The Standby Lounge is a room where aquanauts wait for the final "green light" to proceed with their allotted missions. It has been furnished in soft, restful tones to give aquanauts a last chance to relax and sort out any last-minute problems that may be bothering them. Focal point of the lounge is the three hydraulic chairs which transport aquanauts to their craft.

COMMUNICATIONS ROOM

The Communications Room is the nerve centre of Marineville. Banks of highly sensitive two-way videophones, monitor and de-coding equipment line the room. Constantly manned, the Communications Room receives a never-ending stream of messages from WASP aquanauts and operatives working in all parts of the world.